THE LOST DIARY OF
TUTANKHAMUN'S MUMMY

Another Lost Diary recently discovered!
The Lost Diary of Erik Bloodaxe, Viking Warrior

The Lost Diary of Tutankhamun's Mummy

Dug up by Clive Dickinson

This paperback edition published in 1998.
Published by arrangement with HarperCollins Publishers Ltd.

The author and illustrator assert the moral right to be recognized
as the author and illustrator of this work.

Printed in the United States of America.

10 9 8 7 6 5 4 3 2 1

MESSAGE TO READERS

In January 1878, a tall block of carved stone weighing 205 tons (186 metric tons) and standing nearly 66 feet (20 meters) tall arrived in wet, cold London. For more than 3,000 years this obelisk had been standing—and then lying—in the much nicer climate of Egypt. Cleopatra's Needle, as the obelisk became known, was being relocated in front of the Houses of Parliament. When, however, it turned out to be too heavy to sit there, the stone was erected beside the Thames River—where it can still be seen today.

Workmen putting the obelisk on the Embankment found what looked like a battered old mat stuck to the bottom. During a lunch break they pulled the mat off and discovered that it was actually a bundle of papyrus paper covered in ancient Egyptian writing and pictures.

One of the men decided it would make a useful placemat for his lunch, and for more than a hundred years it lay in his lunch box. This same lunch box eventually turned up in a junk store and was bought by Clive Dickinson. When he opened the lunch box, he found the ancient papers.

Careful study by Egyptologists Dr. Sandy Slippers and Dr. Haventa Klue revealed that what the workman had used to lay his lunch on was, in fact, the writings of one of the most amazing people living in ancient times. She was a queen and seems to have been the mother of the most well-known Egyptian king—Tutankhamun. The bundle of papers was nothing less than the lost vacation diary of Nefertidy, Tutankhamun's mummy. Inside the diary were several postcards, apparently never sent. Extracts from the diary and the postcards that remained intact are published here for the very first time. They give a unique view of life in Ancient Egypt through Nefertidy's eyes as she cruised down the Nile River.

About 1347 BC

THEBES

Well, you could have knocked me down with the most expensive ostrich feather in Thebes when my dear boy told me his surprise! I know he's the Pharaoh and can do whatever he wants—even though he's only nine years old—but even I wasn't expecting this.

I suspected he was up to something. I'd seen him whispering to his little friend Ankhy Pankhy and sneaking glances at me, thinking I hadn't noticed. I overheard words like "out of the way for a long time," and "get lost forever," so I knew he had something planned for me. And then he told me.

"Mummy, you're always telling me how important the Nile River is to everyone in Egypt. Well, I was wondering how you'd like a break—a nice long break—like a cruise all the way down the river to Giza, to see the pyramids."

To be honest, I've never been very interested in the pyramids. Who wants to wander around boring old piles of stones that have been collecting dust for more than 1,200 years? That's what tourists do, as I told Tutti.

"Yes, but tourists don't travel in the royal barge, stopping to stay with their friends and shopping at places like Herrods with other people's money, do they?"

I had to admit that he was right, and the more I thought about it, the more I liked the idea of cruising in luxury, being pampered, and having everything paid for with everyone looking *up* to me for a change. I also wanted to visit my childhood friend Nicenkleen, who lives out at the Faiyûm. And I thought I'd spend a few days in Memphis with Helvis and Preslettiti and shop till I dropped from exhaustion.

That's why I started writing you, dear diary. I know I'm a bit forgetful, and I thought this would help me remember all the wonderful things I'm going to see and do while I'm away. I thought it would be a nice present for Tutti when I get back—whenever that is.

Now, I must go for my bath . . . or is it my wig fitting . . . or my new robe . . . or my lunch? If only someone would invent something that reminds you of all the things you have to do without your having to remember them—but I suppose that's like imagining you could fly through the air from here to Giza instead of going by river.

We do get funny ideas, don't we?

FIVE THINGS
TO DO BEFORE I GO

1. Get a map.

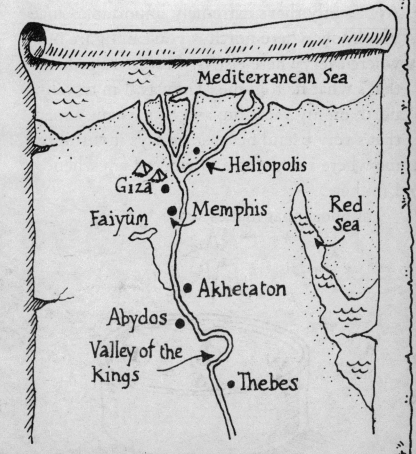

Mediterranean Sea

Giza

Heliopolis

Memphis

Faiyûm

Red
Sea

Akhetaton

Abydos

Valley of the
Kings

Thebes

Tutti gets so angry with me when I make mistakes, especially when I get lost or go the wrong way. So I'm going to be very organized for this trip. One of the nice priests, called Twink Eltwinkel, is helping me. He's very good at finding his way. He knows how to use the stars to find where the north is. Apparently that's extremely important. Once you know where north is you can figure out where everywhere else is. At least I think that's what he told me. Anyway, I'm traveling north on my vacation, and he gave me a map that's very useful because he says it will show me where I'm going and where I am when I'm there.

I suppose that makes sense.

2. **Pray to Hapy.** Hapy, as I learned when I was a little girl, is the god of the Nile. So I must remember to say a few prayers to him if I want to enjoy my trip. I don't want the river to leave me high and dry on a mud bank. Nor do I want an enormous flood that would sweep me down to the Mediterranean Sea.

Of course, Hapy gets quite a lot of prayers, because without HIM we'd all be in the black and sticky, as Tutti would say. Actually that's not quite right, because it's Hapy who brings *wonderful* black mud down the river every year when the Nile floods. That's why we call the soil beside the river "black earth." I've heard that other people don't think much of having their fields covered with black mud, but we ancient Egyptians (and the young ones too) love it because it makes our crops grow marvelously. When the crops grow well there's a good harvest, with plenty to eat, and everyone's happy with Hapy.

I may not be the greatest geographer in Egypt, but I do know the difference between the Black Land and the Red Land. Naturally, I wouldn't dream of going into the Red Land myself. It's a terrible place—wild and empty, with only sand and dust and rocks as far as you can see. There's not a drop of water, so I can only imagine what the people there must smell like if they can't wash! And, as any Egyptian will tell you, smelling nasty is quite sinful. The gods don't like it, and neither do I.

3. Decide when to come back.

Time is something that Tutti and I don't always agree on. He says I have no concept of time. Listening to him, you'd think the most embarrassing thing for a pharaoh is to have a mother who is always in the wrong place at the wrong time. Is that why he's sending me on this trip? Well, I'll let him know exactly when I'm coming back and I'll stick to it, whatever happens. One thing I'm sure about is that I must be back by New Year. No one in Egypt would want to miss New Year unless they were really stupid—or lived out in the middle of the terrible Red Land.

My friend the god Hapy makes sure that New Year always comes at the beginning of summer. He sends a special sign, just in case people like me get confused. At New Year, Hapy makes the water in the river start to rise.

As the water gets higher, the river floods all the fields, bringing that nice thick, black, squishy, sludgy mud that everyone has been waiting for. So I must be back for the New Year celebrations to have that very special mud facepack and to sing "Old Long Nile" with all my friends. I'm not sure that Tutti will think it's a long enough vacation though. It'll only be about forty days and forty nights, and the dear sweet boy wants me to have a *really* long rest.

4. Say goodbye to my old friends.

While the servants are finishing my packing and getting everything ready on the royal barge, I thought I would cross the river and say goodbye to a few old "friends." They're not friends in the way my friends in Thebes are friends. These are rather special. For one thing, most of them are kings. They're also very old. And they're buried underground because they've all gone to their afterlife in the Underworld.

The place where I visit them is called the Valley of the Kings. Tutti will go there one day, although, knowing him, he'll hide himself away and no one will find him for thousands of years.

MEDITERRANEAN SEA

Valley of the Kings → • Thebes Red Sea

I hope that if I visit there often enough I might find a nice place to go myself when the time comes to make my journey to the Underworld. Tutti often says that I should stay in the Valley of the Kings for good—he must think a lot of me to have such a sweet idea.

Thousands of years ago pharaohs and other important people (like me) used to build great big pyramids for themselves. Pyramids are very impressive, but they're not very comfortable. I wouldn't like to spend my afterlife inside one. I know I'd get lost, and the idea of having all that stone piled on top of me gives me the creeps. No, I'd be much happier in a nice cozy rock tomb cut into the hillside, like the ones in the Valley of the Kings. It's a very nice neighborhood too—a very good address when people come to see you.

Of course, there's one tomb there we'd all love to move into. That's the fabulous temple built by a "king" who must have been very much like me—anyway, that's what I think.

This "king" was actually a queen. Her name was Hatshepsut, and she lived only 150 years ago. She showed them who was boss when she ruled Egypt! Oh, yes, they knew who gave the orders when Queen Hatshepsut was running the country. And her temple shows it. It's the first thing you see when you go to the Valley of the Kings. It's very impressive. It would suit me perfectly. I must speak to Tutti about it.

5. Be a good mummy.

It must be the idea of leaving Tutti for a long time that got me thinking about what it takes to be a mummy, and how I must be a *really* good mummy from now until I go away. I guess anyone can be a rotten mummy. To be a good mummy, one that people will still be talking about long after you've gone to the Underworld, takes hard work. Naturally I want to be an extra-special mummy, so I looked up "Mummies" in the Yellow Papyri and found this advertisement:

With an invitation like that, I flew to
Karnak Way like an arrow shot from a bow.
Mr. Rappemtite, the head mummy man, was
very helpful. He showed me some lovely color
pictures painted on the wall and gave me a
brochure that explains everything that has to
be done if I'm going to be a good mummy.

It wasn't quite what I expected, but then so
many things aren't quite what I expect.

Making the Most of the Next Life

At MUM'S THE WORD we know how much we all enjoy life here on earth. That's why we want our customers to get the best from the next life. And take Osiris's word for it, the next life is even better than this one!

MUM'S THE WORD has been sending customers on to the best of afterlives for centuries. With a good mummy that will last forever, you'll know your spirit will have somewhere safe to rest for eternity.

First, we give you a thorough cleaning and take out your innards. (Don't worry, they're put into special jars to stay with you, and we always make sure the heart goes back where it belongs.)

Next comes the drying stage. For forty days our customers are packed in a salt compound—we call it "natron" in the trade. This soaks up all the moisture, leaving you fresh and dry.

When that's over, it's time for another washing and a rubdown with all your favorite spices to give you a heavenly smell your friends will envy until the day they die.

Then we start the most skilled part of the process—the wrapping. Hundreds of yards of top-quality linen bandages are wrapped tightly around you.

It takes two weeks from start to finish, but you can be sure you'll be perfectly preserved for thousands of years to come.

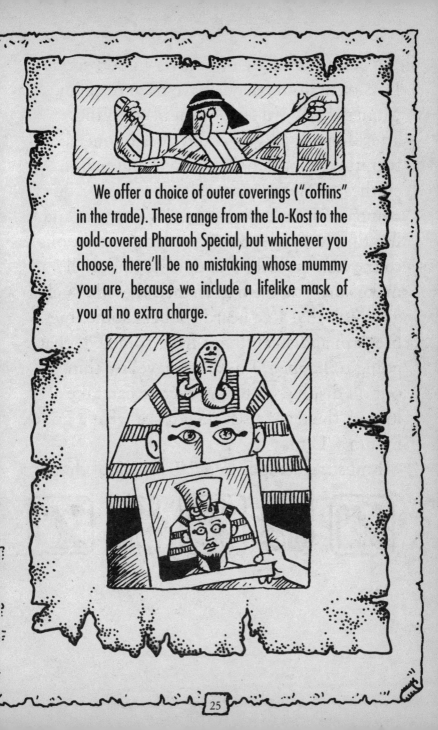

We offer a choice of outer coverings ("coffins" in the trade). These range from the Lo-Kost to the gold-covered Pharaoh Special, but whichever you choose, there'll be no mistaking whose mummy you are, because we include a lifelike mask of you at no extra charge.

You can tell they offer a very good service. Lots of my old friends have been to them. Mum's the Word sends you off into the afterlife with all you could possibly need: furniture, food, boats to travel and fish in, clothes, games to play, statues to keep you company, musical instruments, chariots and hunting weapons, jewelry, even guide books to the Underworld—you name it, they'll make sure you have it. In fact, they do such a good job that I've heard robbers sometimes break in and steal things from tombs. If that's going to happen, I'd rather have my things out on display, so that everyone can take a look at them. At least they'd see what a good mummy I am.

I must remember to tell Tutti about that.

Thebes—last day before my vacation

Thebes is such a nice city to live in. If I wasn't leaving for a fabulous luxury cruise, I'd be sorry to be going away. Of course I'll miss Tutti terribly, and I know he'll be lost without me. That's why I wanted our last day together to be extra special, so I spent the entire day with him—lucky boy.

He has to wake up very early every morning because there's always so much to do. Today, after I rubbed noses with him to wish him good morning, I helped his servants wash and dress him, just like I did when he was a baby. Now he wears the proper clothes of a pharaoh, and he looks so handsome in his little pleated skirt and royal headdress.

He takes his responsibilities very seriously (bless him). The vizier arrived soon after Tutti was dressed and gave a report on all the important things happening in the country. Couldn't he have waited until my little lamb had eaten his breakfast? I've never liked the vizier. He's too big for his boots, if  you ask me, and I've told Tutti so.

"Mum," he always answers, "I can't do it all by myself. I need other people to collect taxes, make the laws work, run the army, feed the people, and keep the gods happy."

Even so, I think he should start the day with a good breakfast.

It still seems strange to think of my little boy as a god. Since he became pharaoh, though, that's what he is, and all the people think he's just as important as the rest of the gods.

Every morning he has to go to the temple to say hello to the other gods and keep them on his side. Amun is the special god. That's why Tutti has his name at the end of his own— Tutankh*amun*. I felt so proud this morning when I watched him go into the temple to make an offering to the great god. I hope he liked it. I wouldn't want Amun to be in a bad mood when I'm sailing down the river.

After the temple, Tutti and I went to school. He pretended to be mad that I was going with him and stamped his foot and said only babies have their mummies with them in school. I think the poor boy was trying to let the other children know just who was king. When he is older, Tutti will have to spend most of his days running the country and greeting important visitors. But for now he still has his schoolwork to do, and it's every parent's duty to help a child get a good start in life by answering all those tricky little questions children ask.

Watching Tutti and the other children

listening to the scribe who was teaching them took me back to when I was his age. The lessons were just as I remembered them. Now I understand what Tutti means about school being boring and repetitive. I thought things might have changed, but they haven't.

Even the stories they chanted aloud were the same ones I had to chant at my school. There must be a better way of learning to read, but I suppose if there were we Egyptians would have discovered it. After all, we are the best in the world at everything.

Tutti's lucky because he can practice writing on smooth sheets of papyrus. That's because he's the king. I feel sorry for the others, who have to make do with pieces of broken pottery or stone slates. Why is writing so difficult? Why can't we invent a machine that does the writing for us? Wouldn't that be marvelous? I had that idea as I watched the children struggling to draw the pictures that Inkyph Ums, the scribe, was teaching them.

I can remember when my scribe tried to teach me to write. First, I had to chew the end of my reed pen until it was bushy, like a paintbrush. Then he made me mix my black ink and my red ink with water, just the way you mix paint. Finally, I had to copy the hieroglyphic pictures. I never did remember them all, and who can blame me? There are more than seven hundred of them! I hope for Tutti's sake his memory is better than mine was.

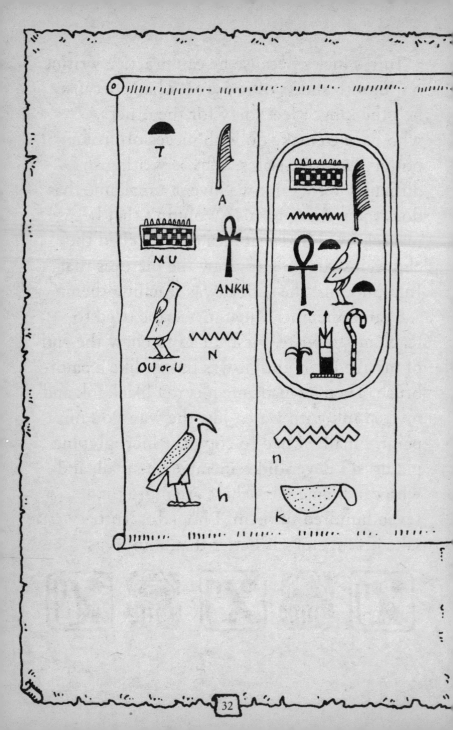

T

A

MU

ANKH

OU or U

N

h

n

k

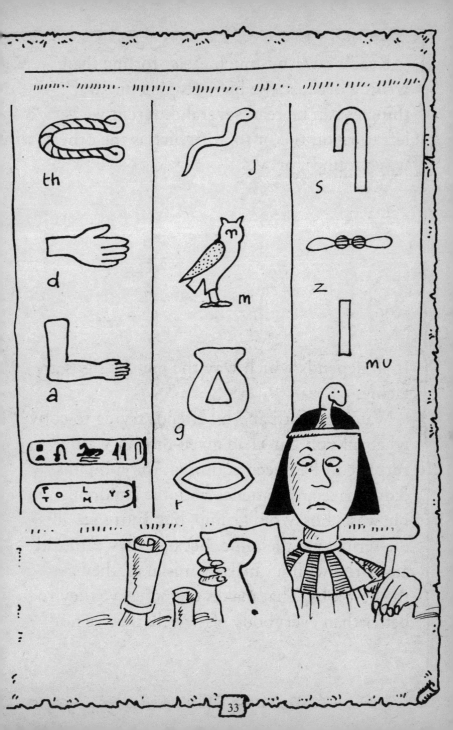

Reading wasn't much easier for me than writing because the hieroglyphic picture thingies can be read several different ways: left to right, tfel ot thgir (which is the other way around), or v
e
r
t
i
c
a
l
l
y.
It all depends which way the picture signs are facing.

Watching Tutti and his friends trying to copy what Inkyph Ums had given them, I wasn't surprised I had been confused. Inkyph Ums didn't have any patience with the children. He was a bossy old grump, but Tutti says all the scribes are the same. Because they can read and write without making mistakes, they get the best jobs. That makes them believe they're better than everybody else. Well, they're not better than Nefertipsy . . . Nefertyped . . . Nefertidly . . . Nefertiny . . . they're not better than me—because I'm the Pharaoh's mummy, and I don't let them forget it!

On the subject of forgetting things, I must remember to take my lumps of charcoal (to make black ink) and that hard red stuff called ochre (to make red ink). Come to think of it, where have I put the reed and palette for writing? . . . Oh, silly me, I'm using them!

What would Tutti say?

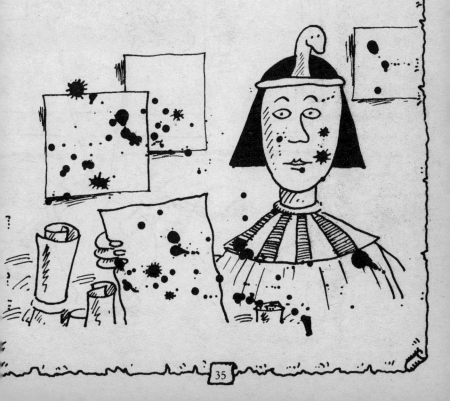

After school it was home for dinner, then I let Tutti play with his toys before going to bed. When I went to rub noses good night, he was sitting up in bed reading a terrifying book called *The Curse of the Mummy's Tomb*. Why he likes these horror stories, I'll never know. He says all the other boys at school are reading them too. Oh well, I suppose it's better than not reading at all.

The Royal Barge
Day 1

Although it was very hard saying good-bye to dear little Tutti, I've now started my cruise, and I can see that this is the *only* way to travel. I know that most people in Egypt travel by boat. A few may have to walk to where they want to go, and there are those dangerous chariots that some rich young men race around in—but no one except me is traveling in such elegant style.

Most of our Egyptian boats have names that say something about them, and this one is no exception. It's called *Tuttal Luxury,* and that's exactly what it is. For one thing, it's not made out of bundles of reeds like a lot of smaller, cheaper boats. Mine is built out of the most wonderful smelling wood. It's called cedar, and it has to be brought from the Byblos, a country around the coast from Egypt where the cedar trees grow to a great height. I have my own cabin to shade me from the sun as I lie on soft cushions and watch the riverbank and other boats drifting past. There are servants to bring me food and drink—beer is my favorite beverage when I'm thirsty. And there are lots of strong young men to row me along, led by the chief rower, Steferedgrafe, who wears a gold medal to show he's the best. Of course the royal barge has a sail,

but I am traveling north, down the river. The wind usually blows the other way, toward the south. So we'll use the sail when we turn around to come back home, up the river.

Now I understand why the hieroglyphic picture thingy meaning "to travel south" has a

picture of a boat with a sail. The picture of a man with oars must mean "to travel north." I feel very pleased with myself for figuring that out. Maybe that's why they say travel broadens the mind.

Abydos

Day 5

After four days' sailing, we've stopped at Abydos, which is a bit touristy because of Osiris. Tutti adores the story of Osiris and his sister, Isis. When I told him about their wicked brother, Seth, who murdered Osiris and cut him into little pieces, Tutti loved it—especially the part where Isis and the god Anubis collected all the pieces of Osiris's body and put him together again to rule the Underworld. Maybe that's why Tutti likes those horror stories he reads now.

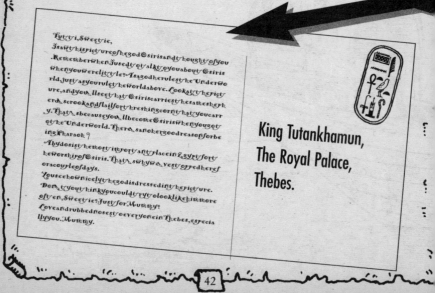

Tutti, Sweetie,

I saw this picture of the god Osiris and I thought of you. Remember when I used to talk to you about Osiris when you were little? I see I'm a god who rules the Underworld just as you rule the world above. Look at the picture, and you'll see that Osiris carries the same shepherd's crook and flail for thrashing corn that you carry. That's because you'll become Osiris when you get to the Underworld. There's another good reason for being Pharaoh?

Abydos is the most important place in Egypt for the worship of Osiris. That's why I've ordered here for a couple of days.

You see how nicely the god is dressed in the picture. Don't you think you could try to look like him more often, Sweetie? Just for Mummy?

Love and rubbed noses to everyone in Thebes, especially you, Mummy.

King Tutankhamun,
The Royal Palace,
Thebes.

Tutti, Sweetie,

I saw this picture of the god Osiris and thought of you. Remember when I used to talk to you about Osiris when you were little? As a god he rules the Underworld, just as you rule the world above. Look at the picture, and you'll see that Osiris carries the same shepherd's crook and flail for threshing corn that you carry. That's because you'll become Osiris when you go to the Underworld. There's another good reason for being Pharaoh!

Abydos is the most important place in Egypt for the worship of Osiris. That's why we've stopped here for a couple of days.

You see how nicely the god is dressed in the picture. Don't you think you could try to look like him more often, Sweetie? Just for Mummy?

Love and rubbed noses to everyone in Thebes, especially you.

Mummy

The Royal Barge
Day 7

I've never been so sick before. Last night I felt as if I were being turned inside out. Nothing would stay down: beer, milk, bread, meat, fish—it was terrible. Luckily there was a very good doctor passing on his boat, and he was brought to see me.

Now, I've had my doubts about doctors in the past. They may be capable of fixing broken bones and healing cuts, but with all the charms and potions they use to treat other things, they seem more like magicians to me. But this doctor, Sawboneandchopit, was obviously the right one for an important patient like me. He asked what I had been eating, and when I said I'd had some bread from the market, he looked thoughtful and asked if there was any left for him to see.

One of the servants brought a piece, which the doctor sniffed and tasted.

"The bread has made you ill, Gracious

One," he told me, in such a nice way.

"But it was baked only yesterday," I said.

"Even so, the flour was not clean." He explained that the baker in the market must have used flour from grain that had been beaten on a floor covered with all kinds of disgusting animal dirt that I can't even begin to describe. Ugh! The doctor didn't seem surprised that my tummy didn't like it. Apparently it's quite common. He told me I should be thankful that at home I eat bread from the royal bakery, which is always spotless. I think Tutti should pass a law to make all flour clean. Otherwise his mummy will have an empty tummy for the rest of her trip.

Dear Tutti, Sweetie,

I couldn't go by this horrible place without sending a card to remind you how pleased Mummy is that you have gone back to the good old ways and the good old gods, unlike naughty Akhenaten when he was Pharaoh before you. The great god Amun must be very pleased too. I can't imagine what Akhenaten was thinking of when he tried to make everyone stop worshipping Amun and start worshipping Aton instead. And as for leaving beautiful Thebes to make a new capital at Akhetaton — well, he must have been crazy. But Mummy's clever boy put a stop to all that nonsense, didn't he? Now you're Pharaoh, we're back in Thebes with the old gods, and I dare say that Akhenaten has joined the mighty Amun in the other life. He doesn't deserve to, after the trouble he caused — it serves him right.

Love and rubbed noses,
Mummy

King Tutankhamun,
The Royal Palace,
Thebes.

Tutti, Sweetie,

I couldn't go by this horrible place without sending a card to remind you how pleased Mummy is that you have gone back to the good old ways and the good old gods, unlike naughty Akhenaton when he was Pharaoh before you. The great god Amun must be very pleased too. I can't imagine what Akhenaton was thinking of when he tried to make people stop worshipping Amun and start worshipping Aton instead. And as for leaving beautiful Thebes to make a new capital at Akhetaton—well, he must have been crazy. But Mummy's clever boy put a stop to all that nonsense, didn't he? Now you're Pharaoh, we're back in Thebes with the old gods, and I don't think Akhenaton has joined them in the afterlife. He doesn't deserve to after the trouble he caused—it serves him right.

Love and rubbed noses,

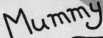

The Royal Barge

Day 10
Moored by the bank

I have just had a very embarrassing experience, and the only one I can talk to about it is you, dear diary.

I feel so silly. The royal barge was brought in beside the riverbank so that the servants could go ashore to buy my lunch. While I was waiting for them to come back, I saw a man on the bank working with a bucket on a long pole. On the other end of the pole was a weight. I was fascinated by what he was doing. First he swung the bucket out over the river and dipped the pole so that the bucket dropped in and filled with water. Then he pushed down on the weighted end of the pole. This raised the bucket back up to where the man was standing, so that he could catch hold of it and pour the water into a nearby ditch that ran into his fields. The work looked quite easy. The weight on one end makes the heavy

bucket feel lighter when it's
lifted. That must save so
much hard labor under
the hot sun when the fields
need water so the crops
will grow well.

I thought this was such
a good idea that I called
over to the man, "What
are you using?"

Now, I may be getting
a little deaf, but I think he
said, "Shut up." Whatever
it was, it sounded very,
very rude.

"What did you say?" I answered crossly.

"Shut up," he said again. I'm sure he did.

That's no way to talk to anyone in a boat as luxurious as mine, and it's certainly no way to speak to the Pharaoh's mummy. So I warned him that if he didn't give me a proper answer, my guards would arrest him.

But he kept on being rude until the soldiers grabbed him and dragged him across to the Captain of the Guard. He was about to cut the worker into little bits of crocodile lunch when the man spoke to him. The Captain of the Guard looked a bit uncomfortable, put his sword away, and came across to me.

"He's been trying to tell you the answer to your question, Your Majesty," he said. "It's a *shaduf*. That thing he's using is called a *shaduf*. Shall I let him go?"

What could I say? What will Tutti say when he finds out? I didn't know where to look. The worst thing was I had to give the man half my lunch as a way of saying how sorry I was.

Tutti, sweetie,

I saw this picture of a crocodile and thought of you. Isn't he looking in its eyes a bit like you? I'm a great people person. What, what you say about me?

The crew on the royal barge keeps a look-out for crocodiles when we are close to the bank or are traveling along a canal leading from the river. I didn't realize how big they are, or how fierce. They have huge teeth. I pointed at his outer one to one of the crewmen, who answered, "All the better to eat you with." He had a funny look in his eye when he said that. The crocodile decided to eat him first.

Love and rubbed noses,
Mummy

King Tutankhamun,
The Royal Palace,
Thebes.

Tutti, Sweetie,

I saw this picture of a crocodile and thought of you. Is it the look in its eyes? Or the way it snaps at people? Isn't that what you say about me?

The crew on the royal barge keeps a lookout for crocodiles when we are close to the bank or are traveling along a canal leading from the river. I didn't realize how big they are, or how fierce. They have huge teeth. I pointed this out to one of the crewmen, who answered, "All the better to eat you with." He had a funny look in his eye when he said that. I hope a crocodile decides to eat him first.

Love and rubbed noses,

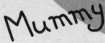

The Faiyûm

Day 12

Thank goodness we've arrived at the Faiyûm. Cruising on the royal barge is very comfortable, but it's wonderful to stretch my legs in this gorgeous house and garden.

Nicenkleen doesn't look a day older than when we were growing up together in the palace. Is her makeup a bit thicker, I wonder? She seems very pleased with her beautiful new house, and who wouldn't be, with a husband as rich and successful as Munnyinthebank?

She's told me so much about living here. Tutti says it is one of the richest parts of the country, so I'm very excited to be visiting the Faiyûm for myself.

For a change I've left the Nile behind and journeyed west, not into the awful Red Land, thank goodness, but to a rich, green, fertile place. Twink Eltwinkel, who gave me the map before I left Thebes, says a place like this is called an *oasis.* All around is dry, dusty desert, but here the land is lower and water comes to the surface to make a huge lake. I think it's heavenly.

Munnyinthebank owns a large estate with many peasants and slaves who farm the land. From my room I can see fields of corn, herds of cattle and goats and pigs, ponds full of fish, and trees full of dates. I won't go hungry here, but I'll have a quiet talk with Nicenkleen about the bread. After what the doctor told me about dirty flour, I can't be too careful.

The Faiyûm
Day 13

Munnyinthebank and I had a very interesting day today. I had thought I would sit around the house chatting with Nicenkleen, eating dates, and trying a wine drink they make from grapes. But he insisted on showing me all around his estate in the hot sunshine. How kind.

He took me to see the fields where the grain grows. I know that bread comes from flour, but I'd always been a bit puzzled about where the flour comes from. The answer is this stuff called grain. The peasants make their bread from a type of grain called barley. I wouldn't recommend eating that. The bread we eat is much nicer. It's made from wheat.

Anyhow, the grain is sown in the fields that have been covered by the Nile mud after the flooding, which starts at New Year. That time of flood is the first season of the year. A nice little peasant told me that—as if I didn't already

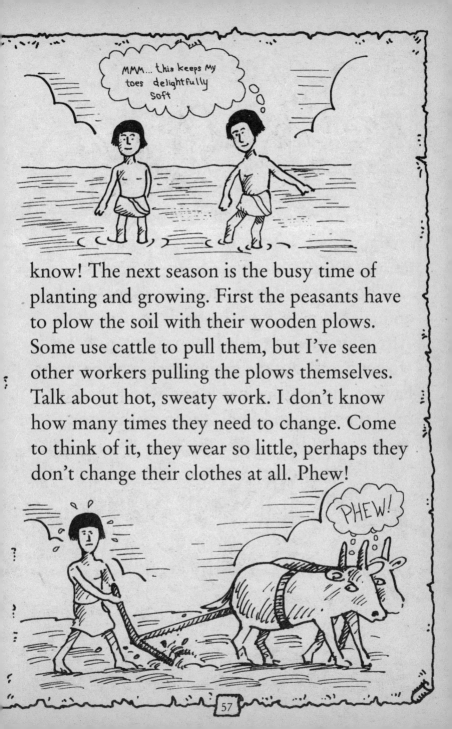

know! The next season is the busy time of planting and growing. First the peasants have to plow the soil with their wooden plows. Some use cattle to pull them, but I've seen other workers pulling the plows themselves. Talk about hot, sweaty work. I don't know how many times they need to change. Come to think of it, they wear so little, perhaps they don't change their clothes at all. Phew!

When the seed is on the ground, herds of animals trample over the fields to press it in. After this there's still a long way to go before we get bread. As the grain grows, the peasants have to dig out the weeds and water the fields until the third and final season of the year.

This is the hot dry part of the year when the grain ripens and the peasants harvest it, cutting the stalks with their wooden sickles fitted with sharp teeth made of flint. The way Munnyinthebank described it, it all sounds so easy. What a shame they can't always keep the grain clean when they thresh it on the floor—not to mention the grit that gets in with the flour. I'm sure chewing gritty bread is wearing my teeth away. When I look at them in my copper mirror, they don't look the same as they used to.

Tutty, Sweetie,

This picture of the peasant sitting in the fields shows you what I've been doing today. I haven't been working in the fields myself of course. That would make me exceedingly hot and sweaty, and I can't imagine what it would do to my clothes. No, Mummy in the chariot has been showing me around his estate and explaining how we grow your food. It's absolutely fascinating. I had no idea.

Did you know bread comes from grain? Anyway, I must talk to you about that when I come home.

Love and rubbed noses,
Mummy

King Tutankhamun,
The Royal Palace,
Thebes.

Tutti, Sweetie,

This picture of the peasants working in the fields shows you what I've been doing today. I haven't been working in the fields myself, of course. That would make me exceedingly hot and sweaty, and I can't imagine what it would do to my clothes. No, Munnyinthebank has been showing me around his estate and explaining how we get our food. It's absolutely fascinating. I had no idea.

Did you know bread comes from grain? By the way, I must talk to you about that when I come home.

Love and rubbed noses,

Mummy

The Faiyûm

Day 14

After yesterday's exhausting tour of the fields with Munnyinthebank, I was so pleased to have a lazy day at home with Nicenkleen.

This new house—villa, I suppose I should call it—would suit me very well. It's so bright and clean, you'd never know it's built entirely of mud bricks. Even the floors and ceilings are made of mud. But everything's covered in paint so you'd never guess.

All around the outside of the garden is a tall white wall. Inside there are trees growing tasty things like dates and figs, and a pool full of juicy fat fish. It's nice to sit here in the shade and enjoy the cool of the day. The roof is flat, of course—at least we don't have to worry about rain in Egypt! So we can sit up there at night.

Nicenkleen has her own part of the house, where the children and other women in the house live too. That's where I'm staying. Munnyinthebank has his private rooms where he does his business, and there are some beautiful big rooms where they have parties and entertain. I suppose the servants and slaves live in the outbuildings. I don't think I want to find out.

All the rooms are wonderfully cool, in spite of the heat outside. Having only tiny windows high up in the walls must help. They let in all the light you need but keep out the hot sun.

What I really like is the furniture. There isn't much—people of our class don't like to be cluttered with lots of furniture—but the pieces they do have must be very expensive. The beds are woven from leather straps that make them very comfortable. I suppose I'll soon get used to the wooden headrest they've given me as a pillow. The chairs have leather straps too, and they are beautifully decorated with carved, painted wood and inlaid with precious metal. I can't imagine how much money Nicenkleen must have spent.

Some of the walls are painted with nice pictures, and others have expensive wall hangings. There's even a special little room where I can go when I "need to go," and a servant cleans out the "need to go" hole in the floor every day so it's never unpleasant in there.

On the north side of the house they've built a shady veranda that catches the cool evening breezes. That's where Nicenkleen and I played a game of senet today. I concentrated really hard on moving my counters around the grid, trying to overcome the obstacles and reach Osiris, but I never seem to win board games like senet. Is it because everyone else cheats? Surely my oldest friend wouldn't do that? Would she?

King Tutankhamun,
The Royal Palace,
Thebes.

Tutti, Sweetie,

You must try the wine they make here. I am bringing jars of it home with me, and I know you will enjoy it. It's quite sweet, which you like. But I think it's even better mixed with honey. You need to be careful how much you drink, though. I think I may have been a little silly when I tried some for the first time.

Munnyinthebank took Nicenkleen and me to the place where they make it. He gave us some to drink while the peasants crushed the grapes with their feet in a big square trough, so that the juice can run out.

Maybe it was the hot sun, but after the peasants had finished pressing the grapes and I had finished quite a few cups of wine, I felt so happy, I decided I wanted to trample the grapes myself. Before anyone could stop me, I had climbed in over the side and was knee-deep in grapes. I must say I was doing just as well as the peasants, only they had been holding ropes hanging above the trough to stay steady and I couldn't reach these. I was so happy, though, it didn't seem to matter—until I slipped and fell over.

Nicenkleen was very understanding when they hauled me out. She says the grape juice color looks good on my dress. I'm not so sure. In fact, I suddenly don't feel very well. I think I'd better lie down, Sweetie. Love and rubbed noses,

Mummy

The Faiyûm

Day 17

I've had a very good visit here, but I'll be happy to get back to the Nile again and continue downriver.

Tonight Nicenkleen has told the cook to give us my favorite things for dinner, so I can't wait to sit down and be brought all kinds of delicious dishes by the serving girls. This is the menu that is being prepared in my honor:

ROAST GOOSE
BOILED BEEF
GRILLED FISH
ONIONS
GARLIC
LEEKS ← lots of it
SWEET PASTRY WITH HONEY
yummy → DATES
POMEGRANATES
FIGS
GRAPES

I suppose Munnyinthebank will give us some of his best wine too. I wonder if I should stick to beer after what happened the last time I drank the wine? I know what Tutti would want me to do. But I am on vacation, so why shouldn't I enjoy myself? Wine it is!

The Royal Barge
Days 18 to 22 (I think)

The last few days seem to have gone by in a haze, and I'm sorry, dear diary, that I haven't written for quite a while. It must have been that last night at the Faiyûm. I remember deciding to enjoy myself and taking an occasional sip of wine, but I don't remember much about being carried on to the royal barge or anything else.

Next stop Memphis and some *serious* shopping.

Memphis

Day 23

After staying in Nicenkleen's fabulous villa, I didn't think anywhere could be better. But this house in Memphis belonging to my old friends Helvis and Preslettiti is almost as big and expensive as Tutti's palace. As the former capital of Egypt, Memphis is where the King used to live. There are lots of big houses in the city, but this must be one of the grandest.

Yesterday evening they gave a huge feast to celebrate my arrival. Helvis is an important official in Tutti's government. He is very rich and powerful, and lots of his rich and powerful friends came to share the feast. I haven't had such a good time in years.

I wore my newest dress, the one I bought especially for banquets like this. It's the latest style, all white and made of the thinnest linen you can buy. There's a very flattering tunic that goes on first, and over this is a full-length gown of beautiful pleated material that hangs from my shoulders right down to my ankles. Since this was an extra-special occasion, I also added a net of red and blue beads across my tunic. It was a little difficult to sit down with this on, but it looked stunning and everyone was admiring my outfit. Tutti would have felt so proud—at least I hope he would.

The other great success of the night was my new wig. I have different wigs to wear for different occasions—as the Pharaoh's mummy I have to look my best all the time. This feasting wig is quite long and has several layers of curls that fall over my shoulders. I think it makes me look like a girl again, though I thought I heard one of the young women giggling to her friend and asking, as she pointed to me, "Who's that old lady wearing the black sheepskin on her head?" I must have been mistaken—this wig is decorated with some of my nicest jewels. It's the height of fashion—at least that's what the wigmaker told me.

It took most of the afternoon to get ready for the feast. In my position you can't leave anything to chance. After I had rubbed myself all over with oil and perfume, it was time for my makeup. As a leader of Egyptian fashion, I use black powder called kohl to put a darker border around my eyes and blacken my eyebrows. Blue eyeshadow suits me best, although some of the other guests looked very striking with green eyeshadow. Red ochre powder gives color to my cheeks, and I use a red ointment to make my lips look just right. Only when I'm completely happy with the way I look in the mirror do I let my servant put the wig on my head.

Then it's time to put the scented cone on top of my wig and go in to the feast. The scented cone is a great idea. When a lot of people—even rich people like the ones Helvis and Preslettiti invited—get together in hot places, there's always a chance the air could start to stink after a while. So we put these perfumed cones on our heads, and during the evening they slowly melt and let sweet-smelling oil run down all over us. That way everyone smells nice all night.

I always feel sorry for the servants and the dancing girls. Their work is so hot, and they can't afford to buy scented cones, so they don't smell too good by the end of the evening.

Of course the servants were very busy bringing us dishes of food and jars of wine and beer. I don't think twice about eating with my fingers in company like this. I'm sure everyone at this feast always washes his or her hands before touching the food.

I had a wonderful time chatting with the women guests and finding out about Memphis. The men sat in a separate group, so I don't know what they were talking about, but I like to think I heard my name mentioned once or twice. One of them told what must have been a joke. He said he'd heard that Tutti had sent me on this cruise hoping I'd be gobbled up by a crocodile or a hippopotamus. All the other men laughed. Apart from that strange comment, it was a very nice evening.

King Tutankhamun,
The Royal Palace,
Thebes.

Tutti, Sweetie,

I know you think I have mush for brains. Well, guess who's been a clever, turned-on mummy? In spite of what you always say, I remembered how interested you are in a new all-girl group of singers and dancers. Memphis is famous for the kind of music that all your subjects enjoy. I suppose that's why they call it country music. Well, I've just been listening to a rather different style of music performed by these girls. It's not exactly my cup of beer, but all the young people here think it's great.

The girls dance and sing at the same time, although I'm not sure they should dance around quite as much as they do, unless they wear more appropriate clothes. Anyhow, the music is played on stringed instruments like lutes, lyres, and harps, accompanied by flutes and other woodwind instruments. The girls keep time with rattles and bells and tambourines. It's very lively, and I know you'll enjoy it when they come to Thebes on their tour.

I wish I could remember what the band is called. Annie Seed and the Swingers? The Coriander Chorus? The Cuminstrels? Nut Meg and the Grinders? The Sweet Girls? I know it's got something to do with spice. Love and rubbed noses,

Mummy

Memphis
Day 25

I don't like sightseeing at the best of times—
and today definitely wasn't the best of times.

I'm sure Helvis meant well when he
suggested I might enjoy spending a day by
myself away from his house, but I can't
believe he had a day like this in mind.

I suppose everyone who comes to Memphis
has to see where the great King used to live.
His name was Narmer, and he made himself
the first Pharaoh hundreds and hundreds of
years ago. Until Narmer took charge, Egypt
was divided into two kingdoms, Upper Egypt,
which is down in the south, and Lower Egypt,
closer to the delta at the other end of the Nile,
where it flows into the sea. Narmer took the
crowns of both kingdoms and made them into
one crown, which all the pharaohs, including
Tutti, have worn ever since.

Memphis is on the boundary between

Upper and Lower Egypt. That's why Narmer built his capital here, and that's why Helvis sent me off to see the sights.

If I had been given a map, I'm sure I wouldn't have had any trouble finding my way around. As it was, I must have gotten slightly lost. It's easy to do. Once you leave the main streets, the lanes between the houses are very narrow (and very smelly), and they all look the same. I'm sure even clever Twink Eltwinkel would get lost without a map.

For one thing, all the houses are the same color, mud brown from the mud bricks. They look identical— little square boxes with flat roofs reached by a staircase. I went inside one and asked the lady who lived there if I could go up onto her roof to see where I was. But when I got up on top, all I could see were lots of other flat roofs and the river away in the distance.

The lady in the house was quite helpful and tried to give me directions. I thought I was being helpful too. She was making bread, and I didn't think the flour she was using looked very clean. So I told her she ought to get some new flour that didn't have animal nasties and dirt in it.

I'm sorry she didn't like what I said. She told me to get lost, which didn't help, because if I hadn't been lost already, I wouldn't have gone to see her in the first place.

It took me hours to find my way out of that maze of alleys. I stumbled into a dark little workshop where a potter was making a pot on a kind of wheel thing he was moving with his hand. Coming in from the bright sunlight, I couldn't see where I was going. Even so, I don't think he should have yelled so loudly when I knocked over the three other pots he had just made.

Then I stumbled upon another little workshop. It was extremely hot, and I could see a lot of smoke. The men inside had almost no clothes on and were drenched in sweat. I tried to ask directions, but they shouted that if I didn't move I'd be a copper statue. I didn't understand what they meant until I saw two of them lifting a big basin full of runny copper off a glowing furnace. Apparently I was standing in front of the molds they were going to pour the copper into. I didn't stay to watch what they did next.

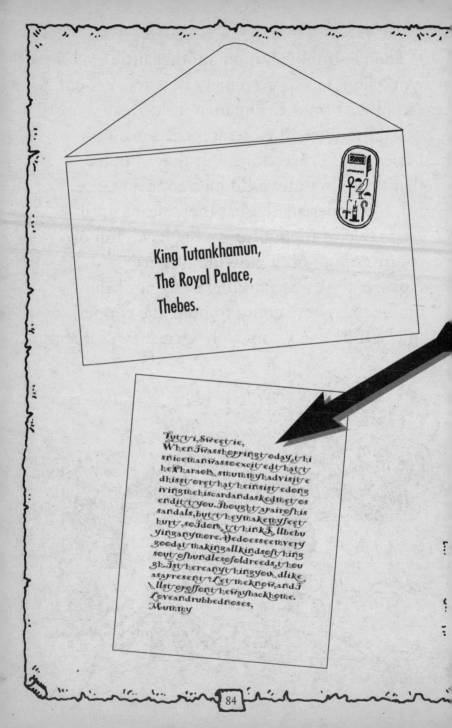

King Tutankhamun,
The Royal Palace,
Thebes.

Tutti, Sweetie,

When I was shopping today, this nice man was so excited that the Pharaoh's mummy had visited his store that he insisted on giving me his card and asked me to send it to you. I bought a pair of his sandals, but they make my feet hurt, so I don't think I'll be buying any more. He does seem very good at making all kinds of things out of bundles of old reeds, though. Is there anything you'd like as a present? Let me know, and I'll stop off on the way back home.

Love and rubbed noses,

Mummy

I saw a lot of people working this afternoon in their cramped little houses—carpenters sawing wood with copper saws and shaping it with copper chisels; men making ropes from leather; weavers making cloth—but none of them could tell me how to get where I wanted to go.

If I hadn't been so exhausted, I would have liked to stay and watch the jeweler who was drilling holes in pretty colored beads to string

WE ALL HAD A "SMASHING" TIME!

them on a necklace. He was using a very fine drill around which he'd wrapped a bowstring that was attached to a bow. When he pulled this quickly backward and forward, the drill whizzed around and made a hole in the bead. The carpenters I saw were using bigger drills for boring holes in wood.

I'd almost given up ever finding my way back to Helvis's house when I spotted a man I thought I'd seen visiting Preslettiti. He was a glass worker, and because things made of glass are only for rich, important people like Helvis, Preslettiti, and me, I was sure he could tell me how to find my way back to their house.

In fact he was very kind and took me all the way there himself. I was so grateful to him that I felt I had to buy something he'd made to say thank you. A glass hippopotamus may not have been my first choice, but he said Tutti would like it very much. I hope he does, and I hope it doesn't get broken on the way home because it was very, very expensive.

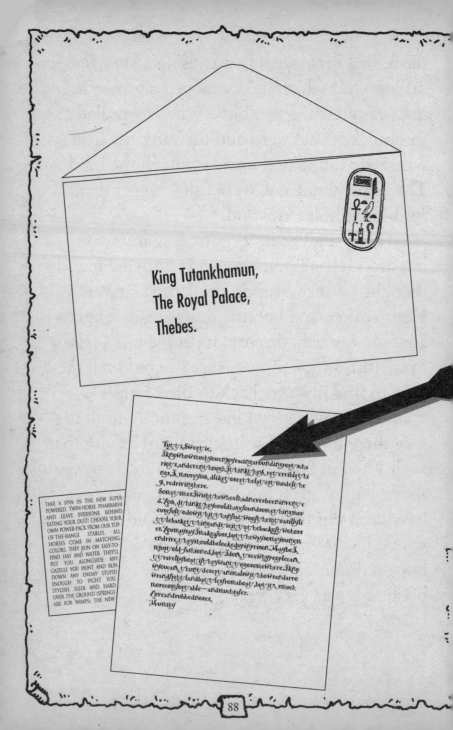

King Tutankhamun,
The Royal Palace,
Thebes.

Tutty i, Sweetie,

I know how much you enjoy racing around in sport chariots, and even though I think they are terrible things, I assure you, I like to see you look at est modestly he a red driving here.

Sometimes I wish the wheels had never been invented. You, d think they could have found something more useful to do with it, an first wheels being easily little basket thing and rieity of the back oft we horses. Young say say I make sure, but they the way some young in end drive, they should be locked up in prison. Maybe I m in just old-fashioned, but I don't see why people can't travel by boat if they want to go somewhere. I know if you can't hunt desert animals with the wrs and fight land but I les from a boat, but it's much more comfortable — and much safer.

Love and rubbed noses,
Mummy

Tutti, Sweetie,

I know how much you enjoy racing around in sports chariots, and even though I think they're terrible things, I'm sure you'd like to see the latest model they're driving around in here.

Sometimes I wish the wheel had never been invented. You'd think they could have found something more useful to do with it than fix two of them to a silly little basket thing and tie it to the back of two horses. You may say I make a fuss, but the way some young men drive, they should be locked up in prison. Maybe I'm just old-fashioned, but I don't see why people can't travel by boat if they want to go somewhere. I know you can't hunt desert animals with bows and arrows and fight land battles from a boat, but it's much more comfortable—and much safer.

Love and rubbed noses,

Mummy

HIPPOPOTAMUS ON THE NILE

Hello, Sweetie,

No medals for guessing what this huge animal is. I just bet Tween-us, I got a little bit muddled and said it was an elephant, but then man I got cross and said it was very old and the very nice little bit it was only an elephant. An elephant hasn't got a round big ears. As you can see, a hippo got a mouth does... t have not got a round has only tiny ears. Otherwise they look very similar. Don't they?

Do you know how much damage a hippo can do when it gets into the fields? I have seen hunters out looking for hippo to stop them from destroying the crops. They see next to me they dangerous. The boat that they use are small, and they have got a tiny killy hit hippos with long spears.

I wonder what hippos taste like? They would certainly be very big. Perhaps we should try one when I get home?

Love and rubbed noses,

Mummy

King Tutankhamun,
The Royal Palace,
Thebes.

Tutti, Sweetie,

No medal for guessing what this huge animal is. (Just between us, I got a little muddled and said it was an elephant, but the man in the postcard shop told me very nicely that it wasn't an elephant. An elephant has a trunk and big ears. As you can see, a hippopotamus doesn't have a trunk and has only tiny ears. Otherwise they look very similar. Don't they?)

Do you know how much damage a hippo can do when it gets into the fields? I have seen hunters out looking for hippos to stop them from destroying the crops. It seems extremely dangerous. The boats they use are small, and they have to try to kill the hippos with long spears.

I wonder what hippo steak tastes like? It would certainly be very big. Perhaps we should try one when I get home?

Love and rubbed noses,

Mummy

Giza

Day 30

We've arrived at Giza at last, and it's very, very HOT.

I suppose the pyramids here are impressive, but it seems a lot of hard work for a lot of people just to build a big pile of stones. Apparently the Great Pyramid that King Khufu built 1,200 years ago is the biggest stone building anywhere in the world. I expect it will always be the biggest. Most people have better things to do with their time.

Still, Tutti has paid for me to come all this way to see the pyramids at Giza, so I'd better appear interested. The guide who showed me around was very enthusiastic. I wish I could remember half the things he said.

The outside of the Great Pyramid is smooth and shiny. That's because it's covered with limestone blocks that the builders polished to make them shine in the sun. The top stone was covered in gold when it was first built—just imagine that. The guide made me take a close look, and I was amazed that all the stones fit together perfectly. I don't think I could have squeezed a sheet of writing papyrus into the gaps between the big stones. It wouldn't surprise me, however, if some greedy people came along and stole these nice smooth stones to build something for themselves.

THE BIGGEST PYRAMID IN THE WORLD—PROBABLY

Underneath the smooth casing stones there are layers and layers of big blocks of stone. The guide says these weigh more than two tons each, and every one was carefully cut and shaped to fit perfectly alongside the others.

Some of the stone came from quarries on the eastern side of the Nile, where the cities are. The pyramids are on the western side, the side where the sun dies at the end of the day. It's to the west that the pharaohs travel when they go to the afterlife, so it's on the west bank of the river that they begin their journey to the Underworld.

The blocks had to be brought across the river on boats. That's easy, though, compared to moving the enormous granite blocks that were used in some places inside the pyramid. They had to come down the river all the way from Aswan, which is even farther upriver than Thebes. I do think some of those old pharaohs were selfish.

To pile the blocks on top of one another, the guide said, gangs of men pulled them up sloping ramps on wooden sledges. There must have been hundreds of blocks on the move at the same time and thousands of men working on the building. I must admit they did a fine job. As far as I can see, the pyramids at Giza are all perfectly shaped from top to bottom, and all four sides look just the same.

The guide says the pyramids are supposed to look like the rays of the sun falling on the earth. I got confused looking at them and trying to remember which direction I was facing. I still think Tutti is better off with his nice rock tomb, and I'll tell him that when I get home. Old Khufu was a show-off if you ask me, although I didn't tell the guide that. I don't think he would have stopped talking even if I had, and I was worn out from walking around and around the three pyramids listening to him ramble on. I'll be glad to get back to the royal barge to cool down and write some more postcards to Tutti.

Lizzy, Sweetie,
Guess what this is. It's the Sphinx at Giza, which I went to look at today. It's a good thing I came when I did. The old Sphinx isn't going to last forever, and I don't know who the who the longer it's going to last. I just get to think of people coming here in a few thousand years and wondering what this big range-shaped lump in front of the pyramids is supposed to be. I must admit I wasn't too sure myself.
You see, I thought it was something else. The head is sort of triangle-shaped, isn't it? How was I to know it was the head of a king? It's really it has the head of a lion. It think someone should have a day all Wit's the culptors who shaped it out of the hill. It could have been as nicely pyramid-shaped head. They aren't it all as big as the three huge ones at Giza.
Love and rubbed noses,
Mummy

King Tutankhamun,
The Royal Palace,
Thebes.

Tutti, Sweetie,

Guess what this is? It's the Sphinx at Giza, which I went to look at today. It's a good thing I came when I did. The old Sphinx is starting to fall apart, and I don't know how much longer it's going to last. I hate to think of people coming here in a few thousand years and wondering what the strange-shaped lump in front of the pyramids is supposed to be. I must admit I wasn't too sure myself.

You see, I thought it was something else. The head is sort of triangle-shaped, isn't it? How was I to know it was meant to look like the head of a king? After all, it has the body of a lion. I think someone should have had a talk with the sculptors who shaped it out of the hill. It could have been a small pyramid instead. They aren't all as big as the three huge ones at Giza.

Love and rubbed noses,

Mummy

Tutty i, Sweetie,

Isn't this a cute little kitty cat? It saw one just like it today when we grassed some men out hunting in the marshes of the Delta, which is where we are now, by the way.

The Nile River divides into several channels here as it flows slowly toward the sea, so there are lots of rich lands for farming and lots of marshes for hunting.

The hunters were after birds that live in the reed beds. The cats frightened the birds into the air, so that the hunters could throw their special hunting sticks at them. It looked almost as difficult as shooting a running gazelle with a bow and arrow from that terrible chariot of yours. I suppose it takes some practice.

Love and rubbed noses,
Mummy

King Tutankhamun,
The Royal Palace,
Thebes.

Tutti, Sweetie,

Isn't this a cute little kitty cat? I saw one just like it today when we passed some men out hunting in the marshes of the Delta, which is where we are now, by the way.

The Nile River divides into several channels here as it flows slowly toward the sea, so there's lots of rich land for farming and lots of marshes for hunting.

The hunters we saw were after birds that live in the reed beds. The cats frightened the birds into the air so that the hunters could throw their special hunting sticks to hit them. It looked almost as difficult as shooting a running gazelle with a bow and arrow from that terrible chariot of yours. I suppose it takes some practice.

Love and rubbed noses,

Mummy

Heliopolis

Day 32

If I see one more tourist site, I think I'll eat my
wig. It was very kind of Tutti to send me on
this vacation, but I'm ready to go home now.
This is the place where we turn around, hoist
the sail, and make our way back up the Nile
to Thebes. We should be home for New
Year—hooray!

This afternoon I've been
brought to look at a tall piece
of carved rock that the people
are extremely proud of. It's
been standing here for a little
more than a hundred years, and
all four sides are covered with
hieroglyphic picture thingies
that I can't read very well.
The top of this tall stone thing
is pointed, and from a distance
it looks to me more like a great
big needle than an obelisk—

I think that's what the guide called it.

I find it confusing trying to keep track of which gods are being praised on this thing, and on everything else that's dedicated to the gods. There are so many gods, that's the trouble.

I don't include Amun, of course. He is the creator god who looks after Tutti and the whole country. But I can't keep the others straight, especially since so many of them have human bodies but animal heads.

There's Anubis, the jackal-headed god who looks after the dead. Toth looks after clever people like scribes and doctors, and he has a bird's head—an *ibis* I think it's called.

Then there's Khnum, who has the head of a ram. He looks after the rough parts of the Nile river called the *cataracts*. Khnum tells Hapy when it's time to make the Nile flood.

Hathor, the goddess of love, has the ears of a cow and the horns of a bull—she's a very odd-looking deity.

There are so many more. Sometimes I'm not sure which god I'm supposed to be thanking or making an offering to. I hope they don't mind too much if I make a mistake now and then.

I don't even know which gods this obelisk was made for. The only good thing about it is that I can lean against it while I write.

If only the sun weren't so hot. It makes me feel so drowsy . . . so sleepy. I think I might close my eyes for a moment. I'll dream of somewhere nice and cool, somewhere far away where the sky is cloudy and it's cold and wet. . . . so sleepy . . . I must make sure I don't let you, dear diary, and all of Tutti's postcards slip down any of the gaps around the bottom of the ob . . . obeli . . . the thing I'm leaning against. That would be too awful. . . .

I must put down my ink and writing reed before I fall . . . before I fall fast . . . Before I fall fast aslee . . .

PUBLISHER'S ADDENDUM

Although the descriptions of life in Ancient Egypt and the facts contained in this diary are accurate, there is no historical evidence that King Tutankhamun had a mummy called Nefertidy, and certainly by the time his "mummy" was found, he was not alive. Nor does it seem likely that there were ever people living in Ancient Egypt with names like Ankhy Pankhy, Twink Eltwinkel, Nicenkleen, Helvis, and Preslettiti.

It seems obvious to us that Clive Dickinson has dug up a hoax. Whoever sold him the lunch box spun a good story. So did the two so-called "Egyptologists," of whom we can find no trace. We only hope that Mr. Dickinson did not pay too much for the lunch box and its phony contents.

Cleopatra's Needle is genuine, of course. It can be seen standing beside the Thames River in London, but the story about the "discovery" underneath it now seems very unlikely.

As publishers we can only apologize and advise our readers not to believe every story they are told when they set out to look for a bargain.

THE REAL TUTANKHAMUN

Tutankhamun ruled Egypt as a boy pharaoh more than 3,300 years ago. He became pharaoh when he was about nine years old, in around 1347 BC, and he died eight or nine years later. He was survived by his wife and childhood friend Ankhesenpaton, and many drawings show that the royal couple grew up to be happily married teenagers.

Although Tutankhamun's reign lasted fewer than ten years and he was still young when he died, historians know far more about his life and reign than they do about many other Egyptian pharaohs because of the discovery of his tomb in 1922. Unlike the burial places of many pharaohs, his tomb had not been seriously damaged by robbers. Howard Carter, the archaeologist who made the discovery, found the young pharaoh's final resting place filled with almost all the objects that had been left with him when he set out on his journey to the Underworld. Among the furniture, clothes, jewels, and everyday objects, Carter found a tiny wreath of flowers—possibly the last farewell offering of the girl queen. But his most spectacular find was the young pharaoh's mummy, complete with its famous gold death mask. This is the only "mummy" of Tutankhamun's about which anyone can be certain, but it is one of the most famous ever to have been found from the days of Ancient Egypt.

And there's another lost diary waiting to be discovered...

THE LOST DIARY OF ERIK BLOODAXE, VIKING WARRIOR

VIKING SCANDAL – GORBLIME TELLS ALL!

Newly discovered diaries and logbook cuttings reveal that the famous Viking king Erik Bloodaxe couldn't write. However, his court poet, Gorblime, could, and he gives astonishing details of life in Viking times.

- Battles and barbarism
- Longships and love
- Births, marriages, and plenty of deaths
- Poems and prisoners
- Erik's victories and his wife's vengeance
- Viking gods and Viking myths
- Travel and adventure

and much, much more.